The Buddhist Cleanse

The 1-Day Spiritual Detox

Nick Keomahavong

Co-Written and Edited By
Phra Michael Viradhammo

CONTENTS

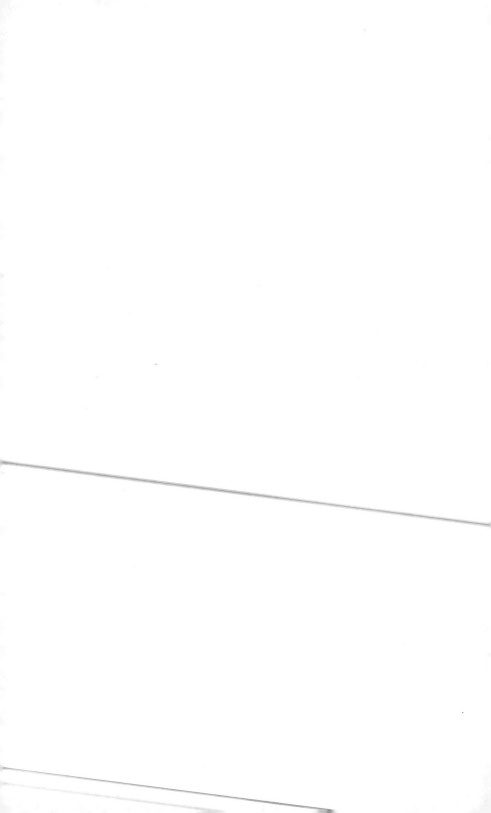

Preface

M y intention with this book is to provide you with a simple, yet profound guide to help you shift your life. If you're looking for a fluffy-lovey-dovey-feel-good book...it's better to look elsewhere. If you're looking for an academic approach to Buddhist philosophy, you won't find that here either. But if you are looking for a life defibrillator, you've found it. The straightforward steps outlined in this book will provide you with the proper jolt to jumpstart the process of genuine change in your life. This 24-hour detox will help you to flush toxicity and purify your insides...no, I'm not talking about a colon cleanse. I'm talking about a spiritual cleanse. The Buddhist Cleanse.

Maybe, at the moment, your life is an absolute mess, and you are in need of a hard reset. Or, maybe, it is the case that something just feels "a little off," and you are seeking to incorporate more balance into your life. Or, perhaps, you are rather content with the state of your life in this moment and would just like to deepen an existing spiritual practice. Whatever the case may be, the Buddhist Cleanse can instigate the change that you are looking for in 24 hours.

After over a decade of experience in the mental health field and after years of experience as a Buddhist monk in Thailand, I have come to realize that the East and West must join forces in order to produce a truly holistic approach to personal transformation. Mental health professionals in the West tend to help clients make changes in their life by conducting talk therapy and interventions. But—from my experience—these interventions can, at times, be disjointed and sporadic. The tools provided for patients are often effective at helping individuals cope with symptoms of their problems, but, more often than not, they fail to eliminate suffering at the root cause of the issue.

Buddhism, on the other hand, identifies the root cause of suffering. The problem is: this wisdom is so deep that it is often difficult for people to properly interpret and practice in daily life in order to transform themselves deeply. And, despite being timeless and universal, this ancient wisdom needs a fair bit of adaptation for people to effectively apply it in a modern context.

This book seeks to do just that. I aim to leverage my experience as a psychotherapist, a Buddhist monk, and a person who has walked his own path of healing in order to synthesize a holistic model to heal suffering at the root cause. The prescription comes in the form of a 1-Day, clear-cut, actionable plan to help you effectively purify your inner world.

This type of guidance is exactly what I wish I would have had as I started my journey of healing and self-transformation many years ago. I needed something to tell me clearly what steps to take and how to take them properly. I needed to understand why it was worth investing my time and effort into this plan. I needed it to be easy to apply. I needed it to be fast. And, above all, I needed it to work.

I am here to tell you that as long as you are willing to work for it, the Buddhist Cleanse will work for you. 2,500+ years of spiritual seekers who have practiced these principles can attest to this. You now have this ancient wisdom in the form of a modern guide. This is my gift to you on a silver platter. Enjoy :)

Benefits of
1-Day Spiritual Detox

- It provides time and space to breathe, reflect, contemplate, and realign
- It resets your life
- It breaks the monotony of your daily routine
- It gets you unstuck
- It gives you an opportunity to slow down your body and mind
- It supports deeper meditation
- It helps you see yourself, others, and your situation more clearly
- It helps you rebalance
- It recharges you
- It connects you back to yourself
- It creates time for self care

- It creates time and space to readjust your priorities
- It helps declutter and reorganize your mental space
- It provides clarity to make new, wiser decisions
- It halts negative momentum
- It initiates positive momentum
- It gives you a chance to do a dopamine-fast
- It reduces interaction with external stimuli
- It helps reverse sensory overload by giving your 5 senses a chance to rest
- It helps you discover or rekindle passion for wholesome hobbies
- It creates a proud feeling from engaging in virtuous behavior

"Ehipassiko"

-The Buddha-
"Come And See"

The Buddha often said this after giving a teaching. He constantly challenged his students to not just blindly believe what he (or anyone else) said. Rather, he said, you must put the teachings to the test of experience in order to verify the truth for yourself.

Introduction

Detox Talk

Nowadays, toxic material continuously attacks and gains entry to your body and mind. The growing popularity and diversity of detoxes on the market is an indicator of this fact. From drug and alcohol detoxes, to detox diets, to the newly-popular digital detox, people are constantly seeking new ways to depollute themselves. Despite the differences in details, every detox shares one essential aspect: they eliminate something harmful from your life.

Drug and Alcohol Detox Centers help patients withdraw from a harmful substance by completely removing the person from their old external environment. This serves to abruptly break their self-destructive patterns. A new, safer, and cleaner environment supports the patient with a combination of medication and talk therapy. Such an environment helps them flush out physical toxins, mental delusions, and unwholesome desires. This process re-wires them. It teaches them a new way of life—a new way of living drug-free.

Detox diet programs, on the other hand, focus on aiding the body in flushing out any toxins that may have accumulated over time. They achieve this through a specific eating or drinking regimen. Whether it's consistently drinking a special juice concoction, eating a select assortment of food, or cutting off food entirely through the process of fasting, these detox diets serve to vitalize the body's natural detoxification processes. On top of introducing healthier alternatives, these new habits of ingestion help people stop introducing harmful material into their body. This type of detox provides the body with the proper conditions to reset, flush itself, and function more effectively.

Finally, digital detoxing has become very popular in recent years. From social media, to entertainment, to dating, to education, to business ventures, to shopping, and everything else in between, our entire world is quickly going digital. This shift has happened so fast that people often find it difficult to control—or don't even realize that they have developed—quite unhealthy relationships with technology. Such mindless consumption leads to addictive behaviors which can contribute to poor physical and mental health. Digital detoxing focuses on limiting or completely cutting off this overstimulation from technology for a certain period of time. There are even centers and retreats committed to creating an environment that jolts people out of their technology-dependent patterns while helping them discover a more balanced way of living.

Again, these detoxes are different in their details, but alike in their essence. They jumpstart the process of change and flush out pollutants from the body and/or mind. And the simple reason that they are so popular is because they work. They are very effective in achieving what they set out to do.

But what about people who are wanting to eliminate toxicity from their lives but can't clearly identify such a specific cause or issue? What if you are just clogged up energetically, stuck in the monotonous routine of the rat race...is there a detox that can help you flush out your stale lifestyle, habits, and patterns?

The answer is yes. But if you really want to incorporate such a holistic shift in a lasting way, you need to reach past the physical body, past the psychological aspect of yourself, and dig deep into the very core of your being. You need to access and cleanse the spiritual dimension of yourself. And this is precisely what this book is designed to do.

The 1-Day Spiritual Detox gives you clear and easy to follow instructions to get your life to move in 24 hours. But before you can get things to move, first you need to learn how to stop. Although this book will list plenty of ideas on how to create positive momentum, its main function is to abruptly halt any negative momentum in your life. Stop first. This is the foundation of change. Stop doing things that are harmful and self-sabotaging in nature. Only then, will you create the space and energy to effectively move forward in the direction you desire.

The 8 Protective Shields

The question is: what do you stop doing? And how could there be a list of things to stop doing that can work for anyone, in any situation, seeking to incorporate any degree of change into their life? For the answers to these questions, we can look to the 8 precepts of Buddhism.

The 8 precepts are a set of guidelines designed to help people meditate to a deeper level and emulate the lifestyle of purity and simplicity followed by Buddhist monks. However, despite arising out of a Buddhist context, it is not necessary to be Buddhist for these guidelines to benefit you. It is not even necessary to have an existing meditation practice. The 8 precepts are universally applicable to anyone who wants to shift their life in a deep way. So, in order to make the name of these guidelines reflect their universal, non-religious nature, we will refer to them from this point onwards as the 8 Protective Shields. This name also points to how these guidelines function as tools to guard your inner world from further toxification.

But, before you can fully appreciate the value of the 8 Protective Shields, it is helpful to understand the Buddhist guidelines for the most basic level of morality: the 5 Protective Shields. And I want to make this clear before moving forward: this information is not an attempt to condemn or make you feel guilty about your current speech and behavior patterns. Nor is it an attempt to persuade you to abandon your current value system and "live like a good Buddhist."

My aim is simply to equip you with the knowledge of how the spiritual dimension of yourself gets polluted and how such pollution affects the quality of your life. I also want to help you understand how these Buddhist guidelines offer an effective method for a spiritual detox. With this information, it is entirely up to you to decide how much you want to change by integrating what you have learned. My aim is simply to help you make a more fully-informed decision.

So, with that disclaimer in place, let's move on to the 5 Protective Shields. With the principle of non-harm to both self and others at its core, the 5 shields constitute a "bare-minimum" code of ethics that helps practitioners avoid "darkening" the mind. What does that mean, exactly...to darken the mind? It means that any time that you engage in any of the activities that the 5 shields advise against (killing, stealing, sexual misconduct, false speech, and consumption of intoxicants) it clouds, dirties, and dulls the quality of the mind.

So, on a personal level, the 5 shields help keep your mind free from the remorse and heaviness of immoral speech and actions. Avoiding such burdening of the mind supports having a clear conscience which consequently leads to perceiving reality with more clarity. On an interpersonal level, the 5 shields function as a framework to preserve basic human rights, reduce conflict, and maintain social harmony. So, with this balance of tending to mental health and maintaining wholesome, considerate relationships, we can see how the 5 shields are universally supportive of a happy, peaceful, and virtuous life.

The 8 Protective Shields, however, are reserved for those who wish to take their practice of inner purification and mental training to the next level. Compared to the original 5, the 8 shields further protect the practitioner from being influenced by distracting and disturbing stimuli from the external world.

So, why would this type of protection be beneficial to someone in the first place? Well, it is important to understand that every sight that you see, every sound that you hear, every scent that you smell, every flavor that you taste, and every sensation that you come into contact with affects your mind in some way. If it is a pleasurable sensation, our instinctual reaction is to try to have more of those experiences. If it is a painful or displeasing sensation, our instinctual reaction is to try to have less of those experiences.

However, just because something looks, sounds, smells, tastes or feels good, does not mean that it is healthy or beneficial to have more of it. Anyone who has had chocolate cake can attest to this. And the opposite is also true. Just because something is not pleasing to our senses, does not mean that it is wise—or even possible—to avoid it. Sometimes, the most challenging situations are the most necessary to face and overcome in order to grow into a better version of ourselves and live a meaningful life.

However, our instincts tend to override this wisdom. Consequently, many of us live our lives trying to maximize pleasurable experiences while doing our best to avoid the not-so-pleasurable ones. This leads to both a lack of satisfaction with the fleeting pleasure provided by sense gratification and a frustration with the inability to escape all the people, places, and things that we do not like. And then we get caught in this cycle of chasing and running away. This leads to our life never quite being where we want it to be. It leads to a persistent lack of contentment and an inability to accept things the way that they are.

The 8 Protective Shields function as tools to quickly interrupt such patterns. They stand guard at the doorways of our 5 senses and stifle the inflow of toxic material. And, if you wield them mindfully, they will shield your inner world from further pollution at the first point of contact.

The 8 Protective Shields are as follows:

1. Refrain from destroying living creatures.
2. Refrain from taking that which is not given.
3. Refrain from all sexual activity.
4. Refrain from false speech.
5. Refrain from intoxicating drinks and drugs which lead to carelessness.
6. Refrain from eating after midday.
7. Refrain from wearing garlands, using perfumes, using cosmetics, dancing,

singing, music, and all other forms of engaging in entertainment.

8. Refrain from lying down on a high or luxurious sleeping place.

Now, I know what you're thinking...dang, that doesn't sound like much fun! Many of those activities have directly created a lot of joy in my life, especially the activities blocked by shield 3, 6, 7, and 8 (...ok, ok, and number 5 too!) And, that's a very understandable reaction. Perhaps, you may also be thinking that this sounds boring. Or repressive. Almost as if this set of guidelines condemns any type of fun or pleasurable experience. And I get that.

But you have to keep in mind the purpose of these shields. Again, the 8 Protective Shields are designed to protect you from being influenced by the external world. They create space between you and the things that you are chasing and running away from. They create space between you and the influence of other people. And this space gives you

a chance to breathe. It gives your senses a chance to rest and recharge. This space abruptly halts the unhealthy relationships you have built with certain sense pleasures such as cravings, addictive behaviors, or self-indulgent patterns. And, finally, it gives you a chance to truly be with yourself.

In this solitary space, you can tune in to what you genuinely need in this moment free from the typical bombardment of distractions from the outside world. By reducing your engagement with external stimuli for 24 hours, you can expose the patterns that have been running on autopilot and actively contributing to your life not being where you want it to be.

And, perhaps, where you want your life to be is very far away from where it is now. Maybe, you are utterly lost and suffering deeply. The 8 Protective Shields will give you the hard reset that you are in need of. Or, perhaps, you just feel a bit stuck in a stale routine. You want to incorporate some positive changes in your life, but you just don't know where to start. The 8 Protective Shields will provide you with the clarity and space to discover the balance you seek. Or, perhaps, you are already moving in the direction you want to be headed in but would just like to take your meditation practice to the next level. The 8 Protective Shields are specifically designed to support a deeper, more effortless meditation practice.

The only prerequisite for this book to be relevant and helpful for you is a desire to change. That's it. Regardless of the details of your situation, the 8 Protective Shields serve as a detox diet for your sensory system. They create the proper conditions and adequate space for your inner world to purify and detox itself. They jolt you out of your old routines and create a new environment conducive to making new, healthier, and wiser decisions. And, at the moment, it may not be clear how each shield achieves these ends. However, after reading each chapter you will have a more thorough understanding of the what's, how's, and why's that might be buzzing around in your head right now.

Book Structure

Each chapter will start off with a simple definition of each shield in both Pali (the ancient language spoken during the Buddha's time in ancient India) and, of course, in English as well. In order for you to clearly understand every activity that falls under each shield, each chapter will provide numerous examples of precisely what things to refrain from. And, finally, each chapter will also explain why each shield is important and how to implement it effectively.

After this, there will be a section that provides you with a big list of activities that you can do in order to utilize this extra time that the shields will provide you with. Since it is likely that many of your previous daily activities will now be off limits, this list will inspire you with new ideas of how to spend your time wisely. This section will be very exciting as it will start to clarify the specific ways in which the 1-Day Spiritual Detox can help you move towards your own personal goals. You can then reference the activities that you identified in this section and plug them into the "build your own schedule" section that follows. This section will guide you through the process of creating your own personal map for a successful, cleansing 1-Day Spiritual Detox.

Finally, there will be a section where you vow to carry each protective shield for the next 24 hours. To make it official, you can copy down the shields, recite the vow aloud, and sign at the bottom. You can even place this sheet in a significant area to remind yourself of the shields that you are now equipped with for the next day.

How To Approach This Guide

The content of this book is presented in a way that allows you to quickly read and easily understand the information. Conceptual knowledge is kept to a minimum and practical steps take the forefront. Given this layout, you could easily read this whole book today and detox tomorrow. No need to go out and buy any special ingredients. No need to wait for a free weekend in your busy schedule. And no need to seek out a guru deep in the jungles of an exotic land. All you need is this guide and 24 hours of time.

However, don't allow the ease and speed with which you can read this book cause you to overlook the importance of proper planning. Take whatever amount of time feels right in order to prepare yourself to have the best 1-Day Spiritual Detox possible. Proper preparation will empower you to fully experience the simple, yet deeply transformative nature of this Buddhist Cleanse. And I would be willing to bet that—after your first spiritual detox—you'll want to come back for more.

And that's a great idea! Whenever you feel unbalanced or that you have gone off course and want to realign yourself, come back to this book. You can revisit this detox over and over again and always discover something new. Why is this the case? Well, it's because each time you revisit this book, you will be approaching it as a new person with a new level of awareness. And each time you guard your sensory system with these shields, you will grow a deeper appreciation for the freedom, clarity, and insight that they provide.

At first glance, the idea of following the 8 Protective Shields for a day may seem dry and boring. You may initially see these shields as limiting your **freedom TO** do certain fun and pleasurable activities. But, after a few times of doing this 24-hour detox, you will experience how these shields provide you with the **freedom FROM** many of the factors that are holding you back from living the life you desire. But, don't take my word for it.

As the Buddha always said with everything that he taught, "Ehipassiko." Meaning don't believe me, but come and practice the teachings for yourself. Only through your own experience can you prove whether something is true or not.

Once you experience the power of the 1-Day Spiritual Detox, it will spark excitement within you as a new world of possibilities opens up to you. You can then funnel that excitement to your family and friends by sharing your experience with them.

Perhaps, you could even challenge them to try the 1-Day Spiritual Detox themselves by nominating them for the #BuddhistCleanseChallenge on social media.

Or, better yet, you can buddy up with them and detox together. This will help you grow stronger and more supportive relationships with the ones you love as you move towards the lives you desire together. Together you will realize how in order to **add** substance to your life, you need to **subtract** the dead-weight that's holding you back first. And, together you can grow a deep appreciation for the concept of how less can be more.

On that note, it's time to wrap up this intro. Again, my intention is to provide you with just enough conceptual knowledge to help you understand the value of this guide. The rest is practical steps and tips to help you effectively shift your life in a quick, yet profound way. I am excited for the things you will achieve through this process, and I am honored to be a part of your journey. So, without further ado, let's get to work.

"Let the discerning man guard the mind, so difficult to detect and extremely subtle, seizing whatever it desires. A guarded mind brings happiness."

"Let a man be watchful of speech, well controlled in mind, and not commit evil in bodily action. Let him purify these three courses of action, and win the path made known by the Great Sage."

~The Buddha~

Protective Shield # 1

Panatipata veramani - refrain from destroying
living creatures.

For the most part, people tend not to have much resistance or confusion regarding this guideline. Don't kill people or animals...ok, got it. But there is a bit more to this than you might assume. Refraining from destroying living creatures includes **ALL** living creatures. This means that swatting flies, slapping mosquitoes, squashing ants, smashing roaches, or harming any other type of household pest is off the menu for today. And, for those who enjoy hunting or fishing, sorry, that would also be on the prohibited list (yes, even if you just catch and release).

Just like all of the original 5 Protective Shields, this shield is helpful to observe at all times even when you are not doing your 1-Day Spiritual Detox. Why? It goes back to the principle of non-harm. When you harm or kill any other being (even if you consider its destruction to be justified or "not such a big deal") it darkens your mind.

Perhaps, you have become callous to this act and don't really notice any twinge of regret or pity towards these pesky creatures. But, upon further reflection, you can see the truth that every creature—no matter how small or annoying—feels pain and flees in the face of death. So, if your aim is to purify your inner world, you must understand that even these seemingly insignificant acts of violence and destruction of life pollute the mind.

"But mosquitoes can spread diseases when they bite you!" claims the typical person seeking to justify their slapping habit. But, unless you live in rural African regions where malaria-ridden mosquitoes roam, this excuse doesn't really hold up. There are always ways around killing. You just have to be a bit resourceful and set up your environment with non-lethal pest repellent methods if they happen to frequent your area.

Here are some tips to help you be more mindful and avoid the destruction of life:

- Use non-toxic bug repellent and cleaners that do not contain pesticides (google this for ideas)

- Use a tiny net to catch mosquitos that are inside and release them outside (this is common practice for monks)

- Just shoo away mosquitoes when they come to have a little snack on your arm

- Keep your living space clean and your food sources securely sealed in order to avoid attracting pests in the first place

There, of course, is a middle way to be found here. It is not advisable to swerve into oncoming traffic in order to avoid a bug hitting your windshield. Accidents happen, and it's important to note that the intention to kill in addition to committing the act is what truly pollutes the mind. So just do your best to be mindful and avoid being too extreme. As you carry this shield both during and outside of your 1-Day Spiritual Detox, your mind will become subtler, and you will gain a greater appreciation and respect for life in all of it's forms.

For the next 24 hours...
I will protect myself with the shield of
refraining from destroying living creatures

Protective Shield # 2

Adinnadana veramani - refrain from taking that which is not given

For the most part, stealing is a universally condemned action. We all know intuitively that it is wrong to take something that doesn't belong to us. And, if you have ever stolen someone else's belongings or ideas, I'm sure you can recall that immediate feeling of uneasiness telling you that it wasn't the right thing to do.

But, beyond the consequences of a guilty conscience, there are also many laws across various societies that protect people's physical and even intellectual property. So, since breaking this rule has physical world consequences in addition to the psychological ones, chances are, you probably already follow this shield pretty well on a daily basis. But, still, we will add a bit more detail of what should be avoided during your 1-Day

Spiritual Detox just in case there are any subtler forms of "taking that which is not given" that you may have overlooked:

<u>Pirating</u> – people often view illegally downloading music, movies, computer programs, etc. as relatively insignificant and justifiable. You may use your logic to justify how artists make a lot of money already or the companies that sell the product you downloaded for free aren't *really* going to feel the effects off of you illegally downloading one itty-bitty pirated copy. Not to mention it's easy to do without being caught or punished. However, even if you get away with online piracy without anyone noticing and you justify it so that you don't feel guilty, it still has a darkening, polluting effect on the mind. And this is what we want to avoid.

<u>Taking credit for someone else's ideas</u> - this can be common in situations where you try to look better in the eyes of others, especially when the owner of the idea is not present.

<u>Taking unmarked items in the refrigerator knowing that it isn't yours</u> - some people have a knack for taking unmarked things inside of the refrigerator at work or home. Even if it is a rule of thumb that unmarked items are fair game at your house or work-place, you should still ask around first in order to avoid refrigerator-related conflicts.

<u>Borrowing without permission</u> - even if you fully intend to bring someone's possession back quickly, there is still a possibility that you will forget to return it, damage it, or put it back in a place where they can't find it.

<u>Taking misplaced items from a public space-</u> - even something as seemingly benign as picking up cash that you found in a public space should be avoided. It is possible that the owner might backtrack to try to find it. And a finder's keepers mentality can cause suffering for someone else. Of course, if it is something like a wallet or purse then bringing it to a local police station or a lost and found can be a considerate course of action.

Here are some tips to help you be more mindful and not commit an act of theft, even unintentionally:

- Always ask before borrowing or eating something that is not yours
- Leave things where you found them in public spaces
- Always give credit to someone else when you use their ideas, even if they are not present when you do

For the next 24 hours...
I will protect myself with the shield of refraining from taking that which is not given

Protective Shield # 3

❧

Abrahmacariya veramani - refrain from all sexual activity.

This is the first shield that gets an "upgrade" from the original 5 shields. Under the 5 Protective Shields, this guideline states to refrain from sexual *misconduct*. Misconduct could come in the form of using trickery or force to compel someone to engage in sexual activity with you. So any form of sexual assault or rape would clearly be considered misconduct.

In addition to this, adultery or being a participant in the act of cheating would fall under this category as well. The wording "being a participant in the act" in the previous sentence is intentional and significant. This means that even if you are not in a relationship, but you engage in sexual activity with someone who you know *is* in a relationship, then that action also falls under the category of sexual misconduct.

When you are aware that the other person is not single and you still decide to engage in sexual activity with them, you intentionally aid someone in breaking a serious promise to another person. And, since such an action can create deep suffering and conflict, this act is considered sexual misconduct and consequently has a darkening effect on your mind. So this is a deeper explanation of shield #3 inside the context of the 5 Protective Shields.

However, for the purposes of your detox, we are interested in the 8 Protective Shields. Therefore, shield #3 gets upgraded to complete celibacy—or refraining from *all* sexual activity.

To understand why this is the case, we need to reconnect with the original intention of the 8 shields. Again, they serve as guidelines to help you reduce distracting stimuli from the outside world so that you have more time and space to focus your energy inwards. Sexual desire is one of the strongest, most primal impulses that a human has. Therefore, seeking to gratify this urge can occupy a large part of our mental space. So, if you can reconnect with the intention of resting your senses, rebalancing, and recharging yourself for a day, you can see how refraining from sexual activity would be very supportive of your inner detoxification process.

So, for the next 24 hours—even if you are in a relationship—sorry...no sexy time for you. Just so you don't get sneaky and try to find a loophole, here is a list of the things that you cannot do: intercourse, oral sex, heavy petting, dry humping...do I really need to go on? Just avoid doing anything sexual with someone else. And, one more thing...you should also avoid doing anything sexual by yourself—in other words you should refrain from masturbation.

In fact, the benefits of not masturbating span well beyond the 1-Day Spiritual Detox. Napoleon Hill talks about "sex transmutation" in his classic bestselling book *Think and Grow Rich.* The general idea is that instead of an orgasm to release your sexual desire, you can funnel that sex drive into a more productive, creative pursuit.

There is even an entire online community or movement called "NoFap" where people abstain from pornography and masturbation. Many "NoFappers" report experiencing transformative benefits as a result. If you are interested, then you can do more research. But, for now, we will just go over a few tips to help you properly protect yourself with this shield for your detox day.

- Clearly communicate with your partner your intentions of celibacy for one day
- Refrain from watching pornographic material
- If you feel an urge to engage in sexual activity, funnel that energy into something else such as
  o Going for a walk

- o Doing some physical exercise: push ups, squats, yoga, etc.
- o Doing an activity from the activity section of this book

Some form of movement can help the urge to pass. And, once it has, you can settle back down into one of the activities that you scheduled for your 1-Day Detox. In this way, you can successfully funnel that sexual energy into something more conducive to your Buddhist Cleanse.

For the next 24 hours...
I will protect myself with the shield of refraining from all sexual activity.

Protective Shield # 4

⟋⟍⟍⟍

Musavada veramani - refrain from false speech

False speech is essentially speech that is dishonest. This type of speech can include telling deliberate lies as well as saying things that you know to be misleading. Sometimes to avoid telling a complete lie, people will tell a half-truth. But, regardless of whether the lie is fully or partially false, the intention to deceive was present.

This deceptive intention is the necessary ingredient for breaking this shield and darkening the mind. Simply saying something untrue due to a lack of proper knowledge—despite being something we all certainly want to avoid—does not break this shield. However, when you intentionally speak in a way that misrepresents the truth, you create a darkness in the mind. In addition, others will likely pick up on your shadiness, thus leading to interpersonal conflict. So, really, nobody wins when you engage in false speech.

However, in order to help support you more fully in your verbal detoxification process, this chapter will cover three other types of "incorrect speech" in addition to false speech. If you can refrain from each of the following forms of incorrect speech for the next 24 hours, you will avoid darkening the mind in a more comprehensive way than if you just avoided false speech in isolation. These other forms of incorrect speech include: divisive speech, harsh speech, and idle chatter (also referred to as pointless speech).

Divisive Speech can include things such as gossiping about others behind their back, intentionally creating conflict between parties, bullying, incitements to violence, and things of this nature. Very simply—divisive speech divides people. It can make the recipients of this speech feel angry, sad, offended, and a large range of other negative emotions. And, despite the enjoyment or excitement that this might create for the one who creates this conflict, it—as you might have guessed—darkens the mind.

<u>Harsh Speech</u> can include aggressive speech and verbal outbursts of rage or anger. It can also include swearing and using coarse language. Some people may not understand how swearing darkens the mind. Many people have accustomed themselves to using swear words in daily conversation. This speech often is not intertwined with anger, and it may be fully accepted by that individual's group of friends. However, this speech can easily offend people who overhear such language. So, even if you have become accustomed to swearing, this habit is one that would be helpful to refrain from for the consideration of those around you and for the consideration of your own mind.

<u>Idle Chatter/Pointless Speech</u> can include speech that lacks depth or purpose. It is speech that does not provide the speaker or the listener with any benefit. These types of conversations are often rambling, incoherent and devoid of any type of

easily discernible value. In more day-to-day language, we can describe people who talk in this way as "talking just to hear themselves talk."

Before we move on to listing practical tips on how to refrain from incorrect speech, it is important to note that expressing any of these forms of incorrect speech through the written word also is a violation of this shield. So, although this shield explicitly refers to speech, writing in a way that is dishonest, divisive, harsh or pointless should also be avoided as it can still darken the mind.

Some tips to support your practice of refraining from incorrect speech are:

- Don't talk so much
- Don't talk so fast
- Take a moment to consider why you are about to speak before you say something
- Don't spark up conversations with people who tend to gossip or frequently draw you into other forms of incorrect speech

- If you notice that you are saying something that isn't true, catch yourself and correct your statement to be reflective of the truth

So much suffering can be created for ourselves and others through the way that we speak. Protective Shield #4 provides you with a powerful framework to help you reduce any harmful speech patterns that you might possess. It may be a bit difficult to apply these principles at first, but don't worry. This is normal.

The good news is: the environment for your 1-Day Spiritual Detox will be more isolative and less social by design. Consequently, refraining from these four categories of speech will be easier, since you will naturally gravitate towards settings where you have less opportunities to communicate with others.

As you apply this mindfulness practice aimed at letting go of harmful speech patterns, just treat it like a game where you try to catch yourself. No need to beat yourself up when you realize that you are breaking this shield. Rather, be kind and compassionate to yourself. Try to change your perspective from one of disappointment or self-criticism to one of excitement. Try to change your perspective to see each instance as an opportunity instead of a mistake.

An opportunity for what? Well, every time you catch yourself engaging in "incorrect speech" in a soft and forgiving way, it is an opportunity to weaken that harmful pattern. Each time, bit by bit, you get to detoxify your inner world. Each instance may seem small and insignificant, but it is the foundation of a deep and sustainable change. With patience and consistency, you can truly transform your entire life. So, do your best to let go of any criticism or frustration that arises. Instead, feel proud of yourself for putting in the effort to incorporate positive change into your life and just enjoy the process like a fun, little game.

For the next 24 hours...
I will protect myself with the shield of
refraining from false speech

Protective Shield # 5

Suramerayamajja pamadatthana veramani -
refrain from intoxicating drinks and drugs
that lead to carelessness

Now, we have made it to the final of the original 5 Protective Shields and also the most widely "struggled-with" shield for Westerners. For many people in Western society, alcohol is simply a part of life. It may have been an integral piece of many fond memories spent with family, friends, and loved ones throughout the years. As a result, many people adopt the attitude of "there's nothing wrong with a few drinks." Although it may have caused a handful of regrettable decisions in the past, for the most part, alcohol has been like a trusty companion that has—time and time again—served as a trusty, social lubricant.

However, there are two main reasons why intoxicants such as alcohol are included in the original 5 Protective Shields. The first reason is that once you start drinking, you become more likely to break all of the previous 4 shields. As your inhibitions lower as alcohol enters your bloodstream, you become less mindful in how you think, speak, and behave.

You are more prone to stretching the truth, gossiping, swearing, and talking in a nonsensical manner. You are more likely to injure or kill another living being, especially if you operate any type of machinery like a car. You are more likely to steal something, even if it is just by accidentally taking something that doesn't belong to you. And, a large percentage of sexual assaults happen in the presence of alcohol. Since it greatly increases your likelihood of breaking the first 4 shields, alcohol is essentially like a gateway drug to darkening the mind through careless speech and behavior.

The second main point is that the mere act of drinking alcohol directly darkens and dulls the quality of your mind. If you've ever gotten drunk, you have experienced this fact first-hand. And, if you personally have never gotten drunk but those around you have, you've experienced this fact second-hand. Your ability to think logically and make wise decisions suffers with every alcoholic drink. You become more emotionally unstable and can swing into states of sorrow or anger very quickly. So that euphoria and social lubrication that you feel from drinking comes at a price.

And, even if you drink a small amount, that dulling and darkening effect of the mind happens at the first drop. Alcohol is the antithesis to clarity of mind. This is the main reason why it should be avoided by those seeking to see their lives more clearly.

Although, we have been talking exclusively about alcohol up to this point, this is not the only substance that can be considered an intoxicant. Any of the following should also be refrained from:

- Marijuana
- Psychedelics including LSD, Psilocybin Mushrooms, Ayahuasca, DMT, MDMA, and so on
- Cocaine, Heroin, or Methamphetamines
- Prescription pills taken recreationally
- Or really any mind altering substance

Ultimately, you should refrain from any addictive or mind altering substance. So, in a best case scenario this would include cigarettes as well. The only substances that are permissible would be prescription or over-the-counter drugs needed for a medical condition and caffeinated beverages. So, for the coffee and tea-lovers out there, no need to fret. You can still have your daily cup of joe. Just do your best to consume in moderation.

Here are some tips to aid you in this process:

- Plan some activities from the activity section to fill up your time in new, drug-free ways

- When you have the urge to drink, smoke or use, replace it with something non-harmful like chewing gum, drinking tea, or doing some physical activity

- Remove alcohol or the substance in question from your house

- Take a break from the company that you drink or use with

For many people, it is difficult to cut out intoxicants entirely from their lives. This is especially the case when most of their social interactions are centered around drinking. And so completely cutting alcohol—or the recreational drug in question—out of your life so abruptly may be very extreme and isolative. Consequently, such a change is not easy to sustain over time. So just start small by refraining from consuming that substance for the 24 hours of your 1-Day Spiritual Detox. The activity section can spark ideas of activities that you can try without the presence of drugs or alcohol.

And who knows...maybe, after some experimentation, you can connect with a new social circle that has more wholesome habits. As you slowly start to lower your consumption, you will enjoy the ability of being able to see yourself, your situation, and those around you more clearly. With this newfound clarity, you will be empowered to orient yourself towards a healthier, happier, sober(er) life.

For the next 24 hours...
I will protect myself with the shield of
refraining from intoxicating drinks and drugs
that lead to carelessness

Protective Shield # 6

Vikalabhojana veramani - refrain from eating at the forbidden time (after 12pm)

If you enjoy intermittent fasting on a regular basis, then this shield will be a piece of cake for you. But, if you enjoy intermittent pieces of cake on a regular basis, then this shield might challenge you a bit.

In most Western cultures, dinner is a big deal. It is usually the meal where we eat the most and spend the most quality time with family and friends. And, although the social aspect of it is nice—if you think about it for a second—it really doesn't make much sense to eat this much food at the end of the day.

After dinner, most people are usually finished with the majority of their work and have already exercised. We really don't need much extra energy at this point. Yet, most of us chow down on our highest calorie meal of the day just a few hours before going to bed. So either a) you go to bed with undigested food sitting in your stomach leading to lower quality sleep. Or b) you seek to burn this extra energy via some not-so-mindful activities that we addressed in the previous chapter. Either one is not so good for your overall health and well-being.

So, although shield #6 of the 8 Protective Shields may prove challenging, this challenge will certainly prove beneficial for you. Fasting from 12pm to sunrise the next morning not only creates numerous health benefits, but it also supports your 1-Day Spiritual Detox in a number of ways.

The first benefit that you will derive from this shield is simply having more time and energy. Planning, buying, cooking, eating, and digesting food is a lot of work. Not to mention you have to do the dishes...or leave them in the sink and get yelled at. Either way, dinner—although delicious—is a taxing event.

And, yes, you might miss out on some social time over your evening meal. But, again, the 1-Day Spiritual Detox is designed to be a day spent largely in introspection. So with the time, energy, and solitude that shield #6 provides you with, you can utilize your evening to perform some of the activities that you will plan from the list at the end of this book.

For those who meditate, this extra time afforded to you by not partaking in the evening meal is the perfect opportunity to clock in those precious meditation minutes. In addition to the extra time, fasting can help you feel much lighter and more energetic in the evening thus leading to a more effortless practice. This is the primary reason why Buddhist monks do not eat after noontime. So, if you want to meditate like a monk, then this is a good place to start.

The question is: how do you deal with the hunger? Well, I have some good news for you. This shield still allows for the consumption of liquids! Now, before you go off and blend up a 16oz steak, hear me out for a second. Although some stricter Buddhist circles may only allow water or tea after 12, we are going to use the more lenient approach to this guideline. Here are some ideas to help you curb your hunger.

- Drink some fruit juice
- Drink some milk—almond or soy for the vegans :)
- Make a light smoothie
    - Pro Tip: try making it before noontime and putting it in the fridge, so you don't get carried away when you are hungry and end up blending up a 3 course meal
- Make a protein shake
- Drink some water and wait a little bit

This last tip actually works really well. If you want to follow this rule a bit more "perfectly" then water can really help you with the hunger urges. What you have to understand about hunger, is that it comes in waves. We might assume that hunger just continues to build over time, but this just isn't the case. Sometimes hunger is your body telling you that you are dehydrated. And so, if you drink some water and wait a little bit, you might just notice that your hunger subsides.

One last tip that can be helpful is communicating your intentions to fast with anybody who you might be living with. You could ask them to avoid cooking food after noontime and possibly eat out that evening so as not to make your practice more difficult.

For the next 24 hours...
I will protect myself with the shield of refraining from eating after 12pm

Protective Shield # 7

◦❧◦

Nacca-gita-vadita-visukkadassana mala-gandha-vilepana-dharana-mandana-vibhusanathana veramani - refrain from dancing, singing, music, entertainment, wearing garlands, using perfumes, and beautifying the body with cosmetics

Ohhhh boy! After seeing that big wall of text above you might feel pretty intimidated. This shield consistently creates the greatest amount of questions and general resistance from people who are introduced to the 8 Protective Shields for the first time. And, understandably so. All of the above activities are extremely common practice for westerners in daily life—except maybe wearing garlands...but if you're into that kind of thing, more power to your flowers!

These activities are not only normal, they characterize a culture. And, again, it's important to note that the 8 Protective Shields are a form of higher mental training. So this shield does not condemn these activities as immoral, but rather, it recognizes them as highly distracting and less than conducive to your 1-Day Spiritual Detox.

The important thing to understand is that all of the activities above are very stimulating to your 5 senses. They release a lot of dopamine(the feel good chemical in your brain). This means that they are fun and enjoyable to experience. But they also draw your attention to the outside world and away from your inner world. Singing, dancing, music, entertainment, garlands, perfume and cosmetics are all either directly designed for or—to some degree—involved in romance and the attraction of attention from other people.

Once again, let's reconnect with the intention of the 8 Protective Shields by using a direct quote from the introduction. The shields "are designed to protect you from being influenced by external stimuli...they give your senses a chance to rest and recharge...they give you a chance to truly be with yourself. In this solitary space, you can tune in to what you genuinely need in this moment free from the typical bombardment of distractions from the outside world."

Often, when we are in a negative head space due to some problem we are facing, we seek out some pleasurable distraction as a "pick-me-up." We distract ourselves with social media, Netflix, YouTube, going to see a movie, singing along to our favorite song, or getting all dolled up and going out on the town with our friends. Although these things make you feel better momentarily, it is not actually providing you with the space that you need to heal. In fact, it is *taking up* more space by *adding more* noise to your life. So, although you feel better after engaging in these activities, they are simply band-aid fixes to a deeper problem. Nothing really changed. You just covered up and distracted yourself from the issue.

To spark genuine change, you need a solitary space with minimal distractions. This is the proper environment that is supportive of seeing yourself and your situation more clearly.

Here is a detailed list of how to properly protect yourself with shield #7:

- Refrain from singing and dancing in any form—this includes humming and whistling as well
  - For the professional shower singers, yes this also includes singing or dancing in your own home where nobody can see or hear you
- Refrain from playing music from any type of device or instrument
  - Even music without lyrics should be avoided
- Refrain from all types of entertainment
  - no movies, no netflix...just chill. Some other things this includes would be going to see shows, playing board games, video games, computer games, apps, and son
- Refrain from using perfumes, cologne or body spray

- o Deodorant is ok if you tend to be a stinky individual, but it should be intended to keep you from not smelling bad as opposed to actively trying to smell good
- Refrain from putting on makeup, hair products, jewelry, or anything that is used to beautify your body or enhance your appearance

For the people who typically take large chunks of time each day to do their hair, do their make-up, and, in general, get all fancy, this shield will actually be great for you. We often hear people say that "true beauty comes from the inside." So embrace that inner beauty and enjoy this 24 hour period as a break from your daily "outer beauty" routine.

Also, one more small note on music: if you happen to be in a public place where music is playing, you don't need to plug your ears and run away screaming. Again, it comes back to your intention. Actively seeking out a place where they play music should be avoided, but if music happens to be playing where you are, there's no need to stress too much.

Important note: this shield is likely changing your current lifestyle dramatically...good. True transformation requires sacrifice. And the sacrifice required by carrying this shield will greatly aid in the process of focusing all of your energy inwards, thus sparking the change you seek.

For the next 24 hours...
I will protect myself with the shield of refraining from dancing, singing, music, entertainment, wearing garlands, using perfumes, and beautifying the body with cosmetics.

Protective Shield # 8

Uccasayana-mahasayana veramani - refraining from lying on a high or luxurious sleeping place.

Disclaimer: for those with physical conditions that require extra support while sleeping, please consult your doctor before adopting this shield.

Congratulations! You've made it to the 8th and final Protective Shield that will support you on your 1-Day Spiritual Detox. The premise of this shield is relatively simple: it helps to keep you from over-indulging in sleep and succumbing to laziness. As one of my teaching monks once wisely said, "when your bed isn't too comfortable, you fight less with gravity in the morning." However, if your bed is a soft, warm, cloud-like fortress, it is very easy to hit the snooze button five or six times and slip back into its pillowy depths.

However, being well-rested is important, so sleeping without a pillow and a blanket on a cold, concrete floor is certainly not what this shield advises. The way to follow this shield properly is to find a middle way approach. The key points for this shield is to make sure that your mattress is low to the ground, thin, and not overly plush. If you do not have a thin mattress lying around, you can craft a modestly comfortable little "nest" on the floor next to your bed. Here are some tips:

- Lay down 1 or 2 thick blankets to create a base
- Sleep with a sleeping bag on top of this base
- If you do not have a sleeping bag, just lay directly on top of the base and cover yourself with another blanket
- Use your typical pillow

This type of set-up is actually more than comfortable enough for a good night's sleep. It's no memory foam mattress, but it is enough to get the job done. The mattresses we have accustomed ourselves to tend to be a bit extra. And, one thing is for sure, they certainly make it easy to overindulge in sleep.

A note on naps: to the serial nappers out there, no need to fear. It's ok to take a nap during the day. However, if you do, try to nap for only 30 minutes or less. Otherwise, your body will enter deep sleep and you will wake up feeling groggy. Plus you don't want to spend your whole detox day sleeping! So again, if you indulge, don't overindulge. Nap in moderation.

For the next 24 hours...
I will protect myself with the shield of refraining from lying on a high or luxurious sleeping place.

How to Make the Most of Your Time

❧

Ok, the painful part is over...now for the fun part. While the 8 Protective Shields may have removed many things from your daily life, this removal has created space for new choices, activities and experiences. Maybe a majority of your typical daily activities are now off limits. This might leave you feeling a bit lost as to how to spend your time. But, have no fear! The big 'ole list below has a bunch of activities that fall inside the bounds of the 8 Protective Shields. Hopefully, this list can inspire you to create a day that you will truly enjoy.

As you scan the list below, observe your initial reaction as you read each bullet point. If you feel a spark of excitement, then jot down what you just read as a "potential self-care activity." During this process, let go of the critical part of yourself that will say, "oh no, no, you—can't do, won't be good at, or won't actually enjoy—that!"

First of all, if you've never done the activity in question before, then you can't be sure of any of those things. And, second of all, being good at the activity in question isn't the point! Trying something new and enjoying the process is the point. And, who knows: if you are brave enough to follow your curiosity, maybe, you'll even find your new passion.

So, read the following list of self care items with an open mind, and take note of what excites you. You can reference this new, condensed list of activities that you are about to create in order to help you plan out your 1-Day Detox during the schedule-building section that follows. So go ahead and arm yourself with a pen or pencil and a piece of paper and get to reading!

- Meditate
- Pray
- Read

- Inspirational, self development, or spiritual texts would be best
- Avoid romance novels, magazines, comic books, etc.
- Journal (*some ideas of what to journal about listed below*)
  - Gratitude
  - Good deeds you are proud of
  - Freewriting/Braindumping
  - General reflection
- Draw Mandalas
- Color in a coloring book
- Make a Collage/Scrapbook
- Listen to or practice chanting
  - Suggestion: look up - Dhammacakkappavattana sutta chanting with subtitles on YouTube
- Listen to recordings of nature sounds
- Sketch
- Go for a walk in nature

- If it's safe, try barefoot!
- Spend time in nature
- Paint
- Play with clay or play doh
- Take Photos
- Knit or Crochet
- Go People Watching
- Go For A Bike Ride
- Do Yoga (go to a class)
- Exercise
- Stretch
- Go for a Swim
- Cook A New Recipe
- Take a Cooking Class
- Write or Read Poetry
- Do Some Gardening
- Trim Your Nails
- Volunteer/Do Community Service
- Make Jewelry
- Get a massage

- Go On a Picnic
- Go for a Hike
- Go for Ice Cream
- Call or video chat family or friends
- Spend time with your kids or partner
- Take a warm bath with salts or oils
- Make a cup of coffee or tea
- Get a pedicure or manicure
- Put on a homemade facemask
- Sleep in
- Take the kids to grandma or grandpas house
- Go to your favorite place of worship
- Go to the park
- Play with your pets
- Prepare a healthy breakfast
- Shave your legs
- Do Nothing
- Go to a Botanical Garden
- Do a DIY Craft Project
- Take a ride around town

- Prepare a healthy meal
- Go grocery shopping
- Donate clothes
- Organize your finances/personal accounting
- Pay your bills
- Have a garage sale
- Create a vision board
- Write a letter
- Do laundry
- Get a haircut
- Write affirmations
- Write goals
- Write plans of action
- Digital Detox (*cut back or refrain from technology usage*)
- Make a healthy smoothie
- Watch the sunrise
- Watch the sunset
- Do a random act of kindness

- o i.e. Buy the persons meal/coffee behind you in the drive thru
- Take a pilates, tai chi, yoga class
- Sit in the grass and watch the clouds
- Surf
- Rock climb
- Kayak
- Build/fix something
- Work on your car
- Detail your car
- Bathe your pet
- Meal prep
- Go to the gym
- Create a sacred space for meditation or prayer
- Make/buy an altar
- Frame pictures of your favorite spiritual or religious figures
- Buy/light nice candles or incense

A Special Note on Cleaning

A lthough the 8 Protective Shields directly clean your inner world, they also free up time and space for you to clean your outer world as well. In fact, both of these actions support each other, which is why the activity of cleaning gets its very own section.

As Buddhist monks, we understand that our physical environment is a reflection of our mind. If you neglect your living space, then it will show up in your mental space. However, the opposite is also true. If you clean, declutter and organize your living space, it will automatically clean, declutter and organize your mental space as well. With that in mind, cleaning might just be one of the most beneficial uses of your time during your 1-Day Spiritual Detox.

Clean and Organize your Bedroom

- Change your bedsheets
- Do all laundry, fold and put it away
- Create a designated space for your keys, wallet, & other important items

Clean and Organize your Office

- Clean your desk
- Organize your drawers

Clean and Organize your Bathroom

- Organize toiletries, clean toilet, empty trash, wipe surfaces

Clean your Closet/Dresser

- Donate clothes you don't wear
- Organize clothes neatly

Clean your Kitchen

- Do dishes, organize kitchenware/cutlery

Clean and Organize your Pantry/Refrigerator

- Wipe down shelves, throw away anything old, organize nicely

Clean and Organize your Car

- Wash outside - body, glass, tires, etc
- Clean inside - wipe down all surfaces, clean glass and windshield, throw away trash, vacuum the floors, declutter and organize center console and glove compartment

Clean your Garage and other Storage Space

- Have a garage sale or donate unneeded things

Declutter and Organize your Computer, Tablet, or other Electronic Devices

- Delete old files
- Organize your files more neatly
- Delete apps or programs you don't use

Depending on the current state of your living space, deep cleaning may take much longer than a day to complete properly. Keep in mind that you can revisit the 1-Day Spiritual Detox as often as you need to. With repetition, your external and internal environment will quickly become much cleaner and more comfortable to live in.

Build Your Own Schedule

Now is the time to take all of the information that you have just learned and create a new life for yourself. It's time to design your destiny!

By utilizing the 8 Protective Shields to stop your negative momentum and using your list of self-care activities to start some positive momentum, you can craft a day that will shift you deeply. It will instigate the change you are looking for and start you down the path to healing. So, in this section, you will create your personalized road map to a successful 1-Day Spiritual Detox.

Below are a few different schedule templates to inspire your planning session. Or, if you would like to create your own unique schedule with different colors, categories, etc., please feel free to do so. These are just some ideas to spark your own creativity.

1-Day Spiritual Detox
Game Plan

To Do List

- [ ]
- [ ]
- [ ]
- [ ]
- [ ]
- [ ]
- [ ]
- [ ]
- [ ]
- [ ]

Reminders

Notes

MY 1-DAY
SPIRITUAL DETOX

TO DO LIST

- [ ] _____
- [ ] _____
- [ ] _____
- [ ] _____
- [ ] _____
- [ ] _____
- [ ] _____
- [ ] _____
- [ ] _____

MOTIVATIONAL WORDS

NOTES

1 Day Detox Plan

Date _____

Time	Agenda	Notes
8		
9		
10		
11		
12		
1		
2		
3		
4		Meal Plan
5		
6		
7		
8		
9		
10		

Taking On the 8 Protective Shields

Now that your day is planned and you are ready to go, it is time to recap and make a vow to take on the 8 Protective Shields for the next 24 hours. If you would like to copy down these shields on another sheet of paper and sign at the bottom in order to make an official contract to yourself, then feel free to do so. Regardless of whether you sign or not, you can make the vow to protect yourself with these shields more official by reading them aloud. If you would like to get started with shield number 8 the night before in order to help yourself be in a "detox mindset" as soon as you wake up, then you can take the vow the night before your detox. However, if you would simply like to follow protective shield #8 on the night of your detox, then you can read and the list below first thing in the morning. Good Luck!

Read the following statement and each shield description aloud:

For the next 24 hours, I vow to protect myself with the shields of...

1 refraining from destroying living creatures	**5** refraining from intoxicating drinks and drugs that lead to carelessness
2 refraining from taking that which is not given	**6** refraining from eating after 12pm
3 refraining from all sexual activity	**7** refraining from dancing, singing, music, entertainment, wearing garlands, using perfumes, & beautifying the body with cosmetics.
4 refraining from false speech	**8** refraining from lying on a high or luxurious sleeping place.

DO NOT READ THE NEXT SECTION
UNTIL AFTER YOU HAVE COMPLETED YOUR
1-DAY SPIRITUAL DETOX

Well Done!

Please Read After Completion of Your Detox

Uh-uh-ahhhhh, I wouldn't read on yet if I were you. If you are peeking at this section before actually doing the 1 - Day Spiritual Detox, I just want to give you one last chance to complete it before reading on. This section will be much more impactful if you do...go ahead. I'll wait for you, I promise :)

(me waiting patiently as I promised)

Welcome back! Now that you have successfully completed your first 1-Day Spiritual Detox, I want to take a moment to say a heartfelt congratulations! I am genuinely proud of you for having the courage to break out of your comfort zone and put in the work to shift your life. Many people will never even consider doing what you just did for the past 24 hours.

But, despite the doubts, the discomfort and the general strangeness of it all, you took action. And, just as the Buddha's words "Ehipassiko" express, taking action and applying the theory is the key to true self transformation.

People can often get wrapped up in theory. They read about Buddhist (or any other) philosophy and it makes them feel good. But, if they don't actually apply that philosophy to change the way they live their life, then nothing much actually changes.

Before applying the 8 Protective Shields and genuinely touching the space and clarity that they provide, the potential benefits that you read at the beginning of this book are simply words on a page. Grasping them intellectually might provide you with momentary satisfaction. However, truly feeling and knowing the depth of these concepts can only be achieved through direct experience. So you should be proud of your courage to act. It means everything.

However, in all likelihood, this first experience with your 1-Day Spiritual Detox was probably a bit rocky and awkward. I just want you to understand that this is very normal. Although the shields themselves tend to be pretty challenging, typically the most difficult part of this detox is knowing how to properly set up your environment to be supportive of your practice.

This is the reason why it is much easier to follow the shields at a monastery or retreat. It is also the reason why withdrawing from an addictive substance is much easier to do at a drug detox center than at home. In either scenario, someone with plenty of experience has already created the environment for you. They know what will support or take away from the effectiveness of the cleansing process, and they set up the surroundings accordingly.

As a new practitioner to the 8 Protective Shields, make sure to honor your current level of experience and know-how. If things did not run quite as smoothly as you had hoped for, don't get discouraged. You have to keep in mind that there is only so much detail that a guide like this can provide you with.

There are many differing nuances to each person's situation that a book could never fully account for. Only repeated practice, observation, and adjustment can provide you with the knowledge necessary to set up your environment in a way that fully honors your very specific set of circumstances.

Take any difficulties that you experienced with your first 1-Day Spiritual Detox as a natural part of the learning process. As with anything that has the potential to be truly transformational, consistent practice is key. If you repeat the Buddhist Cleanse with this type of mindset on a regular (or semi-regular) basis, you will progressively discover your own unique rhythm. As you learn how to properly set up your environment for success, the benefits you reap will grow exponentially.

And, believe me when I say, that you have already taken a huge step in the right direction in the past 24 hours. In case you haven't already done so, I want you to take a moment now to reflect on your experience. Close your eyes briefly and take note of the new energy, space and clarity that this detox has already provided you with. Go ahead. Take a moment to check in with yourself and relive the inner purification you have just undergone.

Perhaps, the change you feel may seem small to you. It may feel as if such a seemingly insignificant shift could not have possibly instigated something deeply profound. But what it has instigated is, indeed, *very* profound. It has instigated the process of healing your suffering at its root cause. And, oftentimes, when people first start walking this path to healing, they tend to have this curiosity and desire to logically understand every aspect of what is happening to them internally.

Let me make this clear: healing does not require intellectual understanding. In fact, most of the time, trying to understand it logically slows down the process of healing itself. The truth is: you don't need to know what's happening in order for the magic to occur. Clarity of the process will come as you continue down your path.

My advice? Just tap into that subtle (or potentially major) shift that you can feel inside yourself as a result of the past 24 hours. Let your intuition be your guide. Allow that feeling of, "dang, I could use more of this" inspire faith in this process of purification.

And, if you need a more logical appeal, remember that the principles within the 8 Protective Shields have stood the test of time. They have helped countless people emulate the lifestyle of Buddhist monks in order to transform themselves over the past 2,500+ years. If you simply focus on your own "inner work," then you will gain access to your inner well of wisdom, and all the answers to your questions will come by themselves. You will as the Buddha said, "become a light unto yourself."

In performing your first 1-Day Spiritual Detox, you have created the critical spark needed for the fires of self transformation to ignite. If you stoke the flame properly, your old, outdated self that no longer serves you will burn and fall away. And out of the ashes will arise a new, stronger, healthier self. You will begin seeing yourself, your situation, and the people around you more clearly. This clarity will empower you to progressively discover and live by your true nature.

I am excited for you to continue on this journey and connect with other kindred souls on this path of healing. Together we will walk hand in hand towards living more fulfilling and fully authentic lives. I hope the positive benefits that you experienced from your 1-Day Spiritual Detox will ripple outwards and positively affect everyone in your life. Thank you for reading, welcome to the family, and I'll see you again in the next book :)

Acknowledgments

First of all, I would like to thank my parents and family. You all have inspired me with your hard work, endurance, loving kindness, patience, and generosity. Your support, encouragement, and belief that a spiritual life is more important than physical world success has enabled me to pursue my own path. I would like to share all my merit from this lifetime with you.

To my teachers—Phra Ajahn Narongchai, Phra Ajahn Burin, Phra Ajahn Pawithai, my meditation teachers and tutors, and other spiritual mentors: I am forever grateful for your guidance, support and encouragement. You have all taught and helped me build a strong foundation for my spiritual life. Thank you for believing in me and giving me the space to grow and mature.

To Phra Michael Viradhammo: thank you for using your writing skills to help my ideas find their proper expression. Without your expertise, eye for detail, and countless hours of drafting and revisions, this book would not be possible. Thank you for believing in me and helping me to bring this book to life. Thank you for being a good kalyanamitta. Thank you for your brotherhood, guidance, and support along this spiritual path. This is only the beginning and I cannot wait to see what the future holds.

To Phra Ekkachai and Phra Tawan: thank you for contributing your photography and editing talents to the design of the cover and other graphics found within the book. The beauty of your work adds an aesthetic that compliments the subject matter of the book perfectly. I rejoice in your merit.

To all my mental health colleagues, supervisors, teachers, friends, monk brothers, clients: thank you for all the support, guidance, and encouragement along the way. You all played a significant part in my journey which led to the creation of this book, so I hope you enjoyed the read and can benefit from the content. There are many more to come!

Connect with the Author

G et a better feel for the broad range of topics, concepts, and stories that Nick has an interest in by visiting his YouTube channel : Nick Keomahavong.

Stay updated with any new resources, products, or other announcements by signing up for Nick Keomahavong's mailing list :

tinyurl.com/nickkeomahavong

About the Author

Nick Keomahavong, previously a practicing psychotherapist, has been ordained as a Theravada Buddhist monk in Thailand since 2018. His books capture his unique perspective by interweaving the tools of the mental health world and the wisdom of Buddhism into simple and practical guides to healing. With a background as a YouTuber and a professional hip-hop dancer, Nick likes to keep it real and deliver his message to the reader with a refreshing, modern flavor. The directness of his writing cuts past the fluff and gets to the point in a way that is relatable and easy to connect with.

Nick has acquired a diverse range of professional experience in the mental health field over the past decade including but not limited to: being the lead clinician at a foster home for over 100 kids aged 12-18, being a program therapist at a drug treatment center in Malibu, California, being a bereavement counselor at a hospice, and being the founder and owner of his private practice True

Nature Counseling Center in San Diego, California.

However, at the pinnacle of his professional success, Nick left it all behind to become a Buddhist monk in Thailand. He wanted to delve deeper into his own healing and become a more refined practitioner of the tools that he was teaching. As he fully focused his energy on becoming more deeply congruent and aligned with his true nature, his understanding of human suffering and how to heal it matured greatly. It is his highest mission to share this knowledge with others in order to help them discover their true nature and live their most authentic lives.